Where's Lorena?

Written by
Rob Waring and **Maurice Jamall**

(with contributions by **Julian Thomlinson**)

Before You Read

to remember

to ride

to wear

beach

coat

child
(children)

doll

fairground

ice cream

lost

smart

stand

television
(TV)

In the story

Alex

Lorena

Mrs. Oliveira

"Dolls are for girls," says Alex. "No. I don't want to play."
His little sister, Lorena, says, "Please, Alex. Let's play."
"No. I don't want to play with dolls, Lorena," Alex says
to his sister.
Lorena says, "Oh, please . . ."
"No, Lorena," says Alex. "I'm watching TV."

Later, Alex talks to his mother. "Mom, I'm going out now," says Alex.

Mrs. Oliveira asks, "Excuse me, Alex?"

Alex replies, "I'm going out now. Can I have some money please, Mom?" he asks.

"Alex," says his mother. "I'm sorry but you can't go out. I want you to stay here with Lorena."

Mrs. Oliveira says to Alex, "I'm very busy today."

"But I want to go out," says Alex.

"Me too! Me too!" cries Lorena. "I want to go, too, Mom."
"Lorena, you're not coming!" says Alex. "Stay here with Mom."
Lorena cries, "But *I* want to go."
"You stay with Mom. You can play with her," says Alex.
He is angry with Lorena. But Lorena is not listening to her
brother. She sits down and starts to cry.

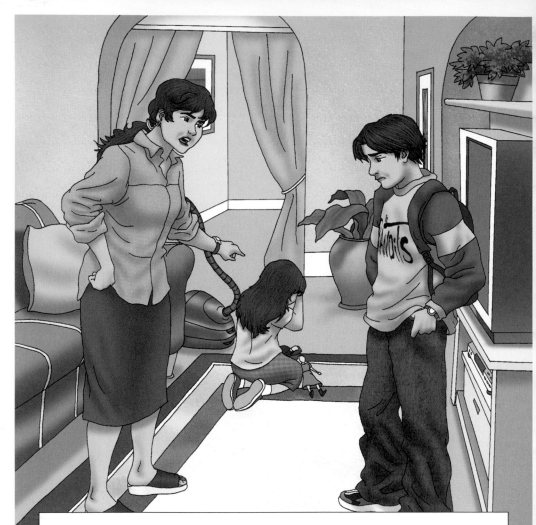

"Look! Stop crying, Lorena. Stop making all this noise!"
says Mrs. Oliveira.
"Okay, Alex. You can go out," says Mrs. Oliveira. "But you
must take Lorena with you."
Alex is not happy. He does not want to take Lorena.
Alex says, "But Mom, I'm meeting Anthony and Mark at
the fairground. I can't take Lorena. She's just a little girl."
"Alex Oliveira!" says Mrs. Oliveira. "Lorena is not *just* a
little girl. She is your *sister*. She is your family!"

"*I* want you to go with your sister," says Mrs. Oliveira.
"Take her with you, or stay here and play with her."
Alex looks at his Mom. "Okay. I'll take Lorena, then," says
Alex. But he is not happy at all.
Mrs. Oliveira gives Alex some money. "Here you are, Alex.
Have a nice time and stay with your sister, okay?" she says.
"Okay, Mom. I understand. Bye," says Alex.
"Good. Come home at 6 o'clock, Alex," says Mrs. Oliveira.
"And don't forget. Don't buy ice cream for Lorena!"

Alex and Lorena often go to the fairground together. But today Alex is angry. He wants to be with his friends. He does not want to be with Lorena. Alex is walking too fast for Lorena. He does not care about her.

"Wait for me, Alex," shouts Lorena. "You're going too fast!"

"Come on, Lorena!" says Alex. "Let's go. Walk faster. Hurry! I'm late!"

Lorena starts to cry. "Alex, be nice to me, or I'll tell Mom," says Lorena. But Alex does not reply.

Alex and Lorena walk through the fairground. There are lots of rides to go on.

"Let's go on this one," says Lorena. She points at a children's ride.

"*The Teacups*? That's for little children!" says Alex. "I don't want to go on *that*! I have an idea. Let's go on this one. *That's* more fun," says Alex. He shows her a big fast ride. Lorena says, "No. Not that one. I get scared on big rides." She starts to cry again.

Suddenly, Alex sees his school friends, Anthony and Mark. He wants to speak with them. He does not want them to see Lorena. "Lorena, wait here," he says. "I'm going to talk to my friends."

"But Mom said . . . ," says Lorena.

"Look. Here. Take this," says Alex. He gives Lorena some money. "Go and buy an ice cream and a drink. Then sit over there and wait for me, okay?" he says.

"But Mom said . . ." replies Lorena.

But Alex replies, "It's okay. Don't tell Mom. Wait at the ice cream stand."

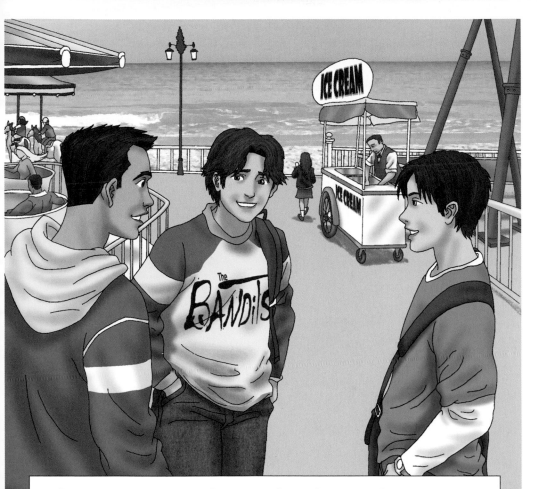

Alex goes over to Anthony and Mark. "Hi, what are you doing?" he asks.

Anthony says, "Nothing much. How about you, Alex?"

"Is Jenny with you?" asks Mark. Jenny is Alex's girlfriend.

Alex says, "No. I'm . . . umm . . . alone." He does not want his friends to see Lorena.

"I'm going home soon. But let's watch a movie later," says Anthony.

Alex says, "Great. Let's meet at The Lagoon at 8 o'clock tonight."

"Okay, see you later," say Mark and Anthony.

Then Alex remembers Lorena. She is waiting for him. "Bye," says Alex. He walks back to the ice cream stand. He looks for Lorena but he cannot see her. "That's strange," he thinks. "Why isn't she here?"

"Lorena? Where are you?" he shouts.

She does not answer. Alex looks around again. He cannot see his sister. Alex walks and walks. He looks everywhere. He shouts out her name. "Lorena! Stop it. Come on. I know you're here somewhere. I'm sorry, okay?" he shouts. But he cannot find Lorena.

Alex is angry now. He walks back to the ice cream stand. "Excuse me," he asks the man. "Did you see a little girl in red here? She's wearing a red coat."

"Yes, I did," says the man. "But she went away. About ten minutes ago."

Alex asks, "Oh? Which way did she go?"

"She walked down to the beach, I think," says the man. "The beach! Water! Oh no!" thinks Alex. "It's dangerous at the beach. I must find her."

Alex runs down to the beach. He is not angry now. He is
worried. He runs up and down the beach. He cannot see
Lorena anywhere.
"Oh no!" he thinks again.
"Lorena!" he shouts. "Where are you? Are you okay?"
He cannot find Lorena. "Oh no! Oh, no!" he thinks.
Lorena is lost. She cannot find her brother. "Where's Alex?
What do I do now?" she thinks.

Alex goes back to the fairground and looks again. He cannot find her. Suddenly, he sees a girl in red. "There she is!" he thinks.

"Lorena, come here," he says angrily. "Come here, now." He is very angry with Lorena.

"I told you to stay here. Why did you move? You bad girl!" he says angrily to Lorena.

The little girl in red turns and looks at Alex.
"Listen, Lorena, I told you to stay . . . ," he starts to say.
Then he looks at the girl's face. It is a girl in a blue
dress. It is not Lorena. It is a different girl!
"Ahhh . . . !" cries the little girl. "Mom! Mom! Help!"
"But . . . but . . . ," says Alex. "Oh no!" he says quietly.

The girl cries more and more. "I'm sorry. I'm sorry," says Alex.
"Please don't cry."
The little girl says, "I want my Mom! Go away!"
"I'm sorry. I thought you were my sister. I didn't mean to
frighten you," says Alex. "I'm sorry."
A woman with long hair runs over to Alex. She is very angry.

"What are you doing?" she says to Alex. "Go away.
Leave my girl alone."
"I'm sorry," says Alex to the woman.
The girl says, "Mom. He was angry with me."
"I'm sorry. I thought she was my sister. My sister is lost.
I can't find her," says Alex. "Your little girl looks like
my sister."
"Oh, I see!" says the woman. "I'll help you find her."

Alex says, "She's wearing a red coat. The same coat as your little girl."

"It's okay. Let's go to the police," she says. "They can find her. She'll be somewhere near here."

"No, thank you. It's okay. I don't want to go to the police. *I* want to find her," says Alex. "She's *my* sister. *I* lost her, and *I* must try to find her. She's only 4 years old."

He goes to look for her again. "I should call the police,"
he thinks. "But then Mom will know I lost Lorena. I'll be in
big trouble. I must find her myself. I'll never do this again."
Alex is very worried. He looks for a long time, but he cannot
find her.

Then he thinks, "She may be hurt. Maybe something bad
happened to her." Alex looks on the beach and in the
fairground again. But she is not there.

He looks in many places. He gets more and more worried. It is getting late.

"It's 6 o'clock," he thinks. "I should go home. I must tell Mom. Oh no! I'm in big trouble now."

Alex is tired from looking for her. He walks home. He is very worried about Lorena. He opens the front door.

"Mom, call the police! Call them now!" says Alex. "Lorena is lost!"

But Lorena is there! She is smiling at Alex. He is very surprised.
"Lorena!" says Alex. He is so happy to see her. "You're here!
Lorena! You're safe. I was so worried about you. I was looking
for you everywhere. What happened? How did you get
home?" asks Alex.
"I know our phone number. I'm a big girl," says Lorena. "I called
Mom, and she called the police. The police officer found me."
"You are a *very* smart girl, Lorena," says Alex happily.

Alex smiles at Lorena. "I'm very sorry, Lorena," he says.
"That's okay, Alex," replies Lorena. "I was bad, too."
Alex says, "It was wrong of me to leave you alone. I'm sorry."
"Yes, Alex, it was," says Mrs. Oliveira. "Never do that again!"
The police officer says, "Well, everything's okay now."
"Not for you, Alex," says Mrs. Oliveira to Alex. "You're not
going out again for a long time," she says.

But Alex is not listening. He is looking at Lorena. He is smiling.
Mrs. Oliveira says, "A friend called you, Alex. His name is
Anthony, I think."
"Anthony called me?" asks Alex.
"Yes," says Mrs. Oliveira. "He said something about meeting
at The Lagoon tonight. But you can't go . . ."
"It's okay Mom. I don't want to meet him," says Alex.
Alex looks at his little sister. "Lorena? Let's play with your dolls."